Twisted Humour Exposed

A catalogue record of this book is available from the British Library

First Edition: September 2004

ISBN: 1-84375-116-X

To order additional copies of this book or other titles by Mary Wood please visit: http://www.upso.co.uk/marywood

Published by: UPSO Ltd
5 Stirling Road, Castleham Business Park,
St Leonards-on-Sea, East Sussex TN38 9NW UK
Tel: 01424 853349 Fax: 0870 191 3991
Email: info@upso.co.uk Web: http://www.upso.co.uk

To Sian
with
my sincere
thanks
for a
Brilliant
website!

Best
regards
Mary x

22/10/04.

TWISTED HUMOUR EXPOSED

by

Mary Wood

UPSO

To mark my 50th Birthday
31 July 2004

and

In Loving Memory of

my father

William Johnstone Beaty
25 September 1920 – 25 May 1984

and brother

Richard Beaty
12 April 1962 – 2 October 1986

Welcome to my third book, at last it's here
Turn the pages, for merriment and cheer
Enjoy its humour; laugh out loud
Share it with a friendly crowd!

Thanks to colleagues, family and friends
Their support for me, it never ends
Reflected in each and every page I write
I treasure them all, day and night!

You, my readers, I treasure too
Special thanks, I extend to you
Indulge yourself; it's a veritable treat
Pass it around to all you meet!

About the Author

Mary Wood (née Beaty) was born on 31 July 1954, and enjoyed a happy childhood on the family farm in rural surroundings on the outskirts of Coventry, Warwickshire. She completed her secondary education in Kenilworth and went on to gain secretarial qualifications in Leamington Spa.

Mary continues to enjoy the country way of life on the farm in Ottringham, near Hull, East Yorkshire, where she has settled with her husband and three children. She works as a senior secretary for a well-known healthcare company, and manages successfully to combine her work, family life and social activities with her love of writing humorous poems.

Over the years, Mary's poems have featured in poetry magazines and numerous anthologies, including three Forward Press Spotlight Poets publications 'Crystal Skies' (2001); 'Vast Skies' (2002) and 'Out of the Shadows' (2003).

This is Mary's third book – Twisted Humour (1998/Revised in 2003) and Twisted Humour Unleashed (2003), are both well worth adding to your collection. She hopes you enjoy Twisted Humour Exposed and will acquire the other books in the series to share with your friends and family.

Mary loves the challenge of working with words to create rhyming verse. She is always on the lookout for new material to transform into an amusing poem that will bring a smile to the faces of those who read her work. Visit Mary's website www.twistedhumour.co.uk for further information and on-line order details.

Contents

TED'S FINAL WORDS

Old Ted lay in hospital, desperately close to death
The vicar stood beside him, as he fought for breath
Frantically, he motioned, for writing tools, in haste
The vicar complied, not a minute did he waste
Ted wrote his final words, then he promptly died
The vicar pocketed the note, pushing it inside
In the sadness of the moment, it quite slipped his mind
Until at the funeral, with many mourners lined
He delved into his pocket, where Ted's final words he
found
Forgotten since that fateful day, recovered safe and sound
As he addressed the congregation, the vicar said of Ted
'He passed to me a note, which I admit I haven't read
I'm sure Ted's final words, in this life, I can share today
As a source of inspiration, I will read them, if I may'
Unfolding the note, he quoted the final words of Ted
'You're standing on my oxygen tube,' horrified, he read!

A BOWL OF JUICY PEARS

A bowl stacked high with juicy pears
The Convent girls would make some theirs
Says Sue to Ann, 'Let's take two each'
But as they get within close reach
A nun booms, 'No, you just take one
God's watching them, now girls move on'
Soon they eye some sweeter fare
Chocolate biscuits to tempt the pair
'Take all you want,' Ann then declares
'God's watching that bowl of juicy pears!'

MOTORWAY MANIAC!

Old Eddie, on the motorway
Answered his ringing phone
'Hello dear,' his wife said
In a caring tone
'Be very careful
I've just heard a news report
There's a maniac on the motorway
Soon he will be caught
He's driving the wrong way
Beware, danger's up ahead'
'It's not just one, there's hundreds'
Her frantic husband said!

DEAD AND GONE

The man knelt at the graveside
Oblivious to all around
'Why did you die?' he cried
His voice intensely profound
The vicar approached, in concern
'For whom do you mourn?' he asked
'Such hurt and pain, I discern
Your grief cannot be masked'
He continued, as the man wailed on
'Is it a child, or parent, who died?
Who lies in that grave, dead and gone?'
'My wife's first husband,' he cried!

A HELPING HAND?

Peter and Paul were fishermen
Cast adrift at sea
Scanning the ocean
For help to set them free
Suddenly a huge hand
Emerged from the deep
They fell back in fright
And landed in a heap!

The hand moved slowly
To the left, and to the right
It repeated this action
Then dropped away from sight
Peter was dumbstruck
His face was pale and grave
Paul said, relieved
'It was just a giant wave!'

HOLY TROUBLE!

Russ and Bill were naughty boys, their parents in despair
Wherever there was trouble, they were surely there
Always in the midst of mischief, crime and strife
Discipline was needed, to succeed in later life
The boys' parents decided to enlist the vicar's aid
Held in high regard, local progress he had made
His stern approach to godliness, they hoped he would instil
A change in behaviour of their little Russ and Bill
'Where is God?' of Bill, the vicar sternly asked
Determined to succeed in this mission tasked
Bill, without his brother, sat quietly, staring into space
The vicar wagged his finger, menacingly in his face
He repeated his question, 'Where is God?' he thrust
Bill remained silent, though inwardly he cussed
Suddenly, he bolted, to hide beneath the stairs
Where Russ found him later, taken unawares
Bill was distraught, Russ could plainly tell
'What happened?' he enquired, 'I heard the vicar yell'
'We're in holy trouble,' Bill explained to Russ
'God is missing, and they're all blaming us!'

PECULIAR LOOKS!

It was a cold and chilly day
Rushing to be quick
Sally delved into her bag
For a moisturising stick
She liberally applied it
To prevent lips becoming sore
Her interview was imminent
The job she should secure
She was well qualified
With credentials to impress
It was merely a formality
Expecting absolute success
But the session was disheartening
She was somewhat baffled too
Receiving peculiar looks
Throughout the interview
She left quite deflated
Arriving home once more
Her daughter appeared
Laughing at the door
'Don't tell me,' she mused
'You didn't get the post
Even though it's obvious
You have more than most
It's a poor Beautician
Who applies her brightest red lipstick
Smeared so very liberally
And vastly over-thick!'

RED TARMAC

Two lumps of black tarmac
In the bar one day
Spotted Red Tarmac
Heading their way
They hid themselves away
Under the cloth of a table
Determined to avoid him
If they were possibly able
This was duly achieved
As Red Tarmac departed
The barman asked the pair
Looking downhearted
'Why were you afraid?
He seemed harmless to me'
'No,' they explained
'He's a cycle-path, you see!'

IDENTITY CRISIS!

The lady approached
As chatty as can be
A stranger in the superstore
It was clear to me.

Under the illusion
She knew me very well
She was quite mistaken
But very hard to tell.

Not pausing for breath
Until I raised my hand
Finally I managed
To make her understand.

She looked embarrassed
Said, 'Sorry,' and withdrew
I continued shopping
Then I joined the queue

But she appeared again
Speaking familiarly
'You'll never guess, dear
What just occurred to me!'

THE BRICKLAYER'S CLAIM

Seeking compensation, the bricklayer's claim fell short
'Poor planning,' he had stated, on the accident report
His injuries were multiple; the Board was quite perplexed
No explanation for the cause, no clues in the text.

The Board then advised, if he wanted to succeed
Full details of the accident, they would duly need
These were forthcoming, all aspects notified
Most serious the claim, but humour hard to hide.

The hapless bricklayer, up six storeys, on a roof
All his work completed, realised he'd made a goof
With fifty bricks too many, he was first to frown
He then devised a plan, a way to get them down.

In a barrel, he would lower them, using a fixed pulley
He secured the rope on the ground, as he checked it fully
Then, returning to the roof, he swung the barrel out
Stacked the bricks in tight, and turned himself about.

Down on the ground, he untied the rope, with caution
To ensure the barrel's slow decline, but it was pure
abortion
He was jerked off his feet, as it began a fast descent
Which shot him up the building, like a rocket, heaven sent!

At the third floor, he met the barrel, dropping like a stone
Which explained his cracked skull and broken collarbone
A nasty cut incurred, as he continued swift ascent
Until the barrel hit the ground, for bricks it wasn't meant!

All fifty fell through, as the barrel base dropped out
Then empty, it rose, which turned the bricklayer about
Hurtling down again, the third floor was the spot
They collided at great speed - more injuries he got!

A fractured ankle on each foot, broken tooth too
Lacerations all over, his body thrown askew
He counted himself lucky, for this is where he slowed
Before landing on the bricks, near the busy road!

He cracked just three vertebrae, but his stupidity was clear
He released the rope, then saw the empty barrel drawing near
The Compensations Board wiped tears from streaming faces
As his last injury recounted a broken leg in several places!

ON REFLECTION

I had a little playmate, who strangely looked like me
Not always could I see her, for that could never be
As a child, we'd meet, in the strangest of places
I was always to wonder at our matching faces.

We'd meet by the riverside, as I peered for fish
Or sight of her, I'd catch, in my shiny dish
Perhaps a shop window, as I passed it by
So often we would meet, my playmate and I.

I'd see her in a puddle, but soon she would be gone
Especially when I stamped in it, with my wellies on
Together we'd pull faces, then we both would smile
Our expressions all in unison - it was our youthful style.

Now the years have passed, and I've reached middle age
Too old for a playmate, I've long outgrown that stage
But, of course, I still see her, and I can comprehend
On reflection, my playmate is still my closest friend!

PEOPLE ARE SUSPICIOUS!

People are suspicious; they think there's something going on
A secret romance between us, which they frown upon
People think we may be lovers, isn't that absurd?
Believing there is truth in the rumours they have heard!

People are suspicious, because we talk and get along
Laugh and share a joke, surely that cannot be wrong?
They think, between us, there's more than meets the eye
Could we persuade them otherwise, either you or I?

People are suspicious; they like to fan the flame
Add fuel to the rumour and pass it on again
Will you, or shall I, tell them, their suspicion offends?
There's no romance between us, we're just the best of
friends!

THE LITTLE PAPER BAG

The little paper bag had consulted the doctor
She'd been feeling unwell, and the worry had rocked her
Tests were undertaken; she was asked to return
Another week later, the results she would learn
The day duly arrived, the doctor diagnosed
She was HIV positive, many questions he posed
The little paper bag fidgeted in disbelief
As his intrusive questions beggared belief
'Did you have unprotected sex?' 'Course not,' said she
'I'm a little paper bag, it's plain to see!'
'Have you shared a needle with another drug user?'
'No, I'm a paper bag, I'm not an abuser!'
'You must have had a jab abroad, or blood transfusion'
'No!' she emphatically denied, resenting his conclusion
The doctor seemed confounded, then his expression
lightened
As realisation dawned, his demeanour brightened
This little paper bag, no more need he harry her
'I know,' he cried, 'your mother was a carrier!'

COME IN NUMBER NINE!

The boating attendant called
'Come in Number Nine'
His young assistant alerted
The issue to define
'We have no Number Nine'
He shouted at the double
'Quick,' cried the attendant
'Number Six must be in trouble!'

THE STUBBORN MAN

The usher in the cinema crossly eyed a man
Sprawled across three seats, he surely faced a ban
She asked him to remove himself, he mumbled but remained
The manager was called, but his position he sustained.

The manager called a policeman to remove the stubborn man
'What's your name?' he asked, and established it was Dan
'Where are you from, Dan?' so patiently he spoke
'The balcony,' Dan groaned, 'I think my back is broke!'

WORSE NEWS

The doctor faced Dale
'I'm sorry to say
I've bad tidings
And worse news to convey'
'What's the bad news?'
Nervously asked Dale
The doctor hesitated
His patient turned pale
'The test results show
You've just one day to live'
'What worse news than that
Could you possibly give?'
The doctor drew breath
He was sad to relate
'The results, I regret
Bear yesterday's date!'

HIS PROMISE

The lawn needed mowing
A prime job for my son
But he gave endless excuses
Why it hadn't been done.

My patience was ebbing
The task must not be delayed
I challenged him crossly
Then a promise he made.

After football, he vowed
He'd undertake the mowing
And trim the edges neatly
His sincerity was showing.

On my return from work
Expecting the lawn to be cut
It was still untouched
The mower shed was shut.

He explained in his defence
About the promise he had made
'Sadly football was cancelled
So the mowing is delayed!'

THE NEWSFLASH

Robbie and his girlfriend were parked in lover's lane
Soft music from the radio issued sweet refrain
As they kissed and cuddled, ardour rising high
A newsflash on the radio made the music die.

For a mad killer, with an evil looking hook
In place of a hand, they were warned to look
Truly deemed a dangerous psychiatric case
Robbie's girlfriend, scared, pleaded home they race.

Robbie was annoyed - what harm could there be?
To stay in lover's lane, no danger could he see
But she insisted no time should they waste
He started the engine and sped away in haste.

Outside his girlfriend's house, Robbie exited the car
He walked round to her side, still irate by far
Then he went to pieces, he trembled and he shook
There, on the door handle, hung a bloodstained hook!

THE CONDIMENTS

'Where are the condiments?'
The diner had to ask
The waitress seemed embarrassed
As she went about her task
She returned to the table
And addressed him with a glare
'Sir, a machine is provided
In the Gents, over there!'

CHEF'S WAY

'There's a hair in my hamburger,' Peter, he cries
The waitress looks on, with little surprise
'I demand,' yells Peter, 'to see where you cook'
'Come,' says the waitress, 'you're welcome to look'
She leads him to the kitchen, immediately he sees
The chef flattening meat, under his armpit, with ease
'That's disgusting,' abhors Peter - the waitress, she tuts
'Then you'll definitely not favour chef's way with donuts!'

THIEVING ACTION

Jenny in the teashop
Bought a chocolate biscuit
With her cup of coffee
She found a place to sit
Opposite on the table
A lady caught her eye
She'd picked up the biscuit
And drew the wrapper nigh!

Jenny was outraged
At this lady's thieving action
She snatched the biscuit back
With adverse reaction
The lady was disgruntled
But left without a fight
Jenny enjoyed the biscuit
Consumed with sheer delight.

When her break was over
She continued on her way
Arriving home exhausted
Much later in the day
As she unpacked her bag
She was intensely mortified
To find *her* chocolate biscuit
Neatly tucked inside!

MOANING, GROANING!

Kenny at the mental home
Walking in the grounds
Heard as he approached
Moaning, groaning sounds
'Seven, seven, seven'
Was coming from a wall
He peeped through a hole
To see who made the call
He was poked in the eye
And staggered back, irate
Then came a moaning, groaning sound
'Eight, eight, eight!'

THE NEW GIRL

The boss challenged the new girl
She was always late for work
He'd heard complaints from others
That she was apt to shirk.

He asked if there were reasons
Why she couldn't arrive when due
Revealing staff had seen her come
Much later than the crew.

The new girl was undaunted
Her boss had only served to bore
Then she deigned to ask him
'May I use another door?'

HIS KANGAROO

The zookeeper was trying to keep his kangaroo inside
Its exceptional jumping skills could not be denied
He woke every morning, invariably to find
His efforts to confine it were madly undermined.

The fencing he erected was never high enough
Adding metres every morning was proving very tough
It never made a difference; he was truly beat
His kangaroo's leaping action signified defeat.

The llama, through the fence, then asked the kangaroo
'How much higher must he build it, to imprison you?'
'Oh,' said the kangaroo, 'the sky's the limit, I am sure
He'll not keep me in until he locks the back door!'

A WEEK EARLY

The new dad passed the Scotsman
In a bustling, moving crowd
'A week early, doing fine'
Was all that time allowed
The Scot was later perplexed
On hearing the baby's name was Ted
'You told me it was a wee girlie'
In puzzled tone, he said!

TARDY HARDY

Hardy was constantly late for work
His boss was fed up with his tendency to shirk
'If you don't shape up you're out of here'
Hardy consulted his doctor in absolute fear
Not wishing to lose his job for sure
He requested some pills to hasten a cure
That night Hardy slept well, waking before the alarm
He arrived early for work, fresh and calm
'Look boss, I'm here early,' he was pleased to convey
'Good,' said his boss, 'but where were you yesterday?'

JAMIE'S DOG

Jamie requested detergent, in the village store
It was to wash his dog; he explained the score
Thickly caked in mud, he needed powerful stuff
Grocer Michael warned, "This detergent is tough
It's too strong, I think, to use on your pet
It could be harmful, or kill even yet'
Nevertheless, Jamie bought the detergent and left
He returned weeks later, saying he was bereft
The dog had died; grocer Michael was upset
Having highlighted the hazards of washing his pet
'The detergent didn't kill him,' Jamie assured Michael
'I think it was probably my washer's spin cycle!'

JOHN'S PITTANCE

John was attacked by a mugger in the street
He fought hard with flaying arms and feet
The mugger was powerful, it soon became clear
John was losing the battle, though devoid of fear
The mugger claimed his reward of just twenty-five pence
John's pittance surprised him, thinking him dense
He couldn't resist asking, as they caught breath
Why John fought so hard, to the point of death
For just twenty-five pence, too much effort, he insisted
Brushing himself off, John said, 'The reason I resisted
Was not for the pittance, but I thought you knew
I've got fifty pounds in the sole of my shoe!'

THE DRUNK

The drunk staggered into a pub
The landlord waged war
'You're not drinking in here
You don't need any more'
The drunk tottered out
But within minutes was back
Through a side door he'd entered
To the bar making track
'You're not welcome here'
The landlord repeated
He led the drunk to the exit
Once more he retreated
Minutes later he returned
Entering from the back
The landlord losing patience
Fed up with the flak
Grabbed him by the collar
And escorted him out
'Go home,' he barked
With menacing clout
The drunk looking perplexed
Had a vital point to clear
'Do you own *all* the bloody pubs round here?'

DRUNKEN CHARGE!

She staggered from the pub
As drunk as could be
'Taxi man,' she called
'Might you be free?'
The driver in his cab
Inviting this fare
Nodded his head
But she gave him a glare
'You're drunk,' she accused
Her words were slurred
'I can tell,' she said
'Your face is all blurred!'

STAYING HERE!

Gerry had a room reserved
At a small hotel
Arriving very late
He loudly rang the bell
From the top floor window
As the clock struck two
A lady sleepily called
'Who the devil are you?
What do you want?
It's so late in the night'
Gerry looked up
As the cold started to bite
'I'm staying here,' he said
Impatiently tapping his foot
'Stay there then!' she retorted
Slamming the window shut!

GETTING DIVORCED!

An elderly devoted father
With children living abroad
Rang his son in Canada
Out all his troubles he poured
'Your mother and I are divorcing'
He was calling to say
Peter was shocked and saddened
Expressing utter dismay
'Tell your sister too'
His father went on to request
Peter then rang Australia
At his father's behest
Jenny was stunned at the news
'Leave it to me,' she said
'I'll sort the situation'
Promptly using her head
She put in a call to her dad
'You can't divorce, do you hear?
Peter and I will fly home - do nothing
Do I make myself clear?'
Their father hung up smiling
He turned to his devoted wife
Jubilantly he embraced her
Kissing the love of his life
'Right that's easily sorted
The kids are set on their way
They'll be home for Christmas
And no fares do we have to pay!'

THE TROUBLE WITH KEYS!

Sue was a typist, in Housing she worked
A council position, in which she clerked
She erred when her finger hit the wrong key
Mistyping a 'k' instead of a 'b'
She'd written to a lady whose flat was vacated
With no keys returned, as her contract had stated
But fear in the lady, Sue's letter instilled
'If the keys aren't returned, you'll have to be killed!'

ON AIR

The radio DJ on air
Transmitted every day
Entertaining his listeners
In a new and different way.

He'd introduced a fun slot
Using a mobile phone
Deposited in a public place
Unattended and alone.

Today it was neatly lodged
Between the carrots and peas
In a busy supermarket
For a laugh, and a tease.

He rang the number on air
And waited in anticipation
'Hello,' answered a woman
After nervous hesitation.

'Hello,' greeted the DJ
'Who could you possibly be?'
'I don't know,' came the reply
'It's not my phone, you see!'

EMMA'S ASSISTANCE

Grandma's car was loaded
With bags in the back
She asked little Emma
To help her unpack
Propping up her stick
She started to sort
Each bag in the car
For Emma to transport.

When all bags were unloaded
Grandma turned round
Little Emma's assistance
Had been efficient and sound
This was quite evident
As Grandma could tell
She'd taken the bags
And her stick as well!

FIXING HER FACE!

Little Robbie was playing
In the garden one day
His mum was fixing her face
As he called her way
A hairy brown caterpillar
In the grass he had spied
'Mum, you've dropped an eyebrow'
He helpfully cried!

POOR KEN!

At Ken's school reunion, he observed the other men around
With expensive suits, and bulging stomachs, to expound
To his wife, he proudly commented that no one could dispute
He'd be the only one who'd still fit his graduation suit
His wife eyed with envy the obvious affluence of the men
'You're the only one who has to,' she cruelly snapped at Ken!

DEAD CURIOUS!

Two mates, on a bench, in the graveyard, were sat
Enjoying a smoke, and a cosy chat
Four black-clad pallbearers passed them by
They were carrying a coffin, shoulder high
They passed them once, they passed them twice
In awe, the mates watched, as they passed them thrice
Dead curious, one asked, 'What's up with that lot?'
The other surmised, 'They've clearly lost the plot!'

RAZOR SHARP!

Sarah's mother was invited for dinner at her pad
Her lodger, she noted, was a handsome young lad
Convinced John must be more than a lodger to her
She asked Sarah if her suspicions were fair
Sarah denied all, 'John's just the lodger,' she swore
Her mother left after dinner, saying no more
The next day, John's razor could not be found
Missing since Sarah's mother had called round
Sarah doubted her mother would take such a thing
She promised she'd ask, and gave her a ring
'Mum, I'm not suggesting you took the razor, of course
But John says it's gone missing,' she stated with force
'I'm not suggesting you sleep with your lodger, my dear'
Her mother's jubilant tone was patently clear
'But if John had slept in his own bed last night
He'd have found his razor – I knew I was right!'

TRISH'S FISH

The sound of digging, little Trish's neighbour heard
He peered over the fence, his curiosity stirred
'What are you doing?' The scene was grim
'My pet goldfish has died, I've just buried him'
Tears were streaming down Trish's young face
As she piled the last of the soil in place
'That's quite a big hole you dug there, Trish
Considering the size of your little fish'
Trish gave the mound one last mighty pat
'That's because,' she cried, 'it's inside your cat!'

MOTH TREATING!

Paul had a problem
Professional help was needed
He called to see the vet
With precious time impeded
'I keep thinking I'm a moth'
He informed the busy vet
'I'm sorry I can't help
It's a doctor you should get
Why come here?' asked the vet
'You know it wasn't right'
Paul said, 'I was passing
And attracted by the light!'

HOPE ON A ROPE!

Five men and a woman on the end of a rope
Dangling from a helicopter, there was only one hope
They decided one must let go to save the rest
The rope was weakening, the woman knew best
'I'll give up my life to save yours,' she said
Hanging precariously, upwardly tilting her head
'Women are used to giving things up, sacrificing all
For their men folk and children, on constant call
It's the least I can do, what do you say?'
From the end of the rope, she looked their way
It was a touching speech, the men applauded with claps
Never underestimate the power of a woman, chaps!

THE WC

An English lady planned to settle
In a pretty village in Wales
She'd found a quaint cottage
But left without details
She hadn't seen a WC
Which caused her some concern
So she wrote to ask the agent
Its location she must learn
The agent was quite baffled
He asked the priest's advice
What these initials stood for
The priest's answer would suffice
'Wesleyan Chapel, of course
What else could it be?'
The agent was most grateful
'I'll write back,' he said with glee
'Dear Madam, we have a WC
Some thirteen miles from here
It's only open twice a week
But it's popular, that's clear
Many people go there
If lucky, they get a seat
Early arrival is advised
But standing room's a treat!
I understand it's unfortunate
If, in the habit, you may be
Of going fairly regularly
But some take lunch, or tea

They often make a day of it
Others go by car
If they're hard-pressed
It's a quicker trip by far!
If you wish to pay a visit
I suggest it's on a Sunday
The organist goes every week
Especially to play
The acoustics are excellent
On that I give my word
Even the most delicate sounds
Can easily be heard!
A bell has been erected
On the WC, which rings
Every time someone enters
Such a joy it brings
We're holding a fete soon
To raise some funds to buy
Plush new seats for our WC
God knows how much we try!
I hope I've answered your query
And if you'll let me know
When to Wales you're coming
The WC I'll show
I'll save a seat right next to mine
Of that you can be sure
Yours faithfully
A Jones
PS: The hymn sheets hang behind the door!'

THE MAN IN THE QUEUE

A teacher smiled warmly at the man in the queue
Confused and uncomfortable, he asked, 'Do I know you?'
'I think so,' she replied loudly, with a toss of her head
'You're the father of one of my children,' she said!

GOING NOWHERE FAST!

Hospital Casualty was as busy as could be
Mick was waiting impatiently, with an injured knee
Sitting in a wheelchair, time was dragging so
In a queue for treatment, the process very slow.

After two hours of waiting, Mick eyed a nurse he knew
'Thank goodness, Mrs Cleaver, I'm so glad it's you
I'm fed up with waiting, can you hurry things along?
I'll stay a few more minutes, then I'm planning to be gone!'

Nurse Cleaver smiled kindly and urged him not to fret
Suggesting he remove his trousers, a blanket she would
get
To speed up the process, this idea he favoured too
He trusted her to help him quickly jump the queue!

Mick's trousers removed, Nurse Cleaver's smile was sly
As she took them from him and tossed them shoulder high
'Now Mick,' she said, 'without these you're going nowhere
fast
You must wait your turn - on the list I know you're last!'

GATHERING MOSS!

A blind man on the kerbside, led by his guide dog Moss
With oncoming cars, the road was hazardous to cross
Suddenly, without warning, the dog forged ahead
Dragging the blind man with him, dangerously they sped
Brakes screeched loudly, as cars took evasive action
Just missing the pair, by a hair's breadth fraction
When safely on the pavement, the blind man turned to
Moss
Offering a biscuit from his pocket, but a driver at a loss
Called, 'Don't reward your dog after what's occurred
You were nearly killed, your action's quite absurd'
'No,' replied the blind man, 'I know what I'm about
Just trying to establish which end I need to clout!'

THE JAR OF LIFE

A professor demonstrating to his Philosophy class
Placed several golf balls into a giant jar of glass
He asked, 'Is it full?' They unanimously agreed
He then tipped in pebbles, the students taking heed
As they slipped through the gaps, filling every nook
The professor again invited his students to look
'Is the jar now full?' Of course, they all agreed
Next he poured in sand, filling chinks with speed
They watched amazed, now convinced the jar was full
But he produced two beers; on which they were to mull
He poured the beers into the jar, until both were spent
'Now,' he said, 'Please understand, a lesson is meant
This jar represents your life; the golf balls are the main
The things that are important, the ones that would remain
If all else was lost, your life would still be full; your health
Partner, family, children, friends, in these you have wealth
The pebbles represent your job, your house, your car
Other things that matter, but secondary by far
The sand is everything else, all the minor stuff
If you put the sand in first, that would be tough
No room for the pebbles, or golf balls too
The same goes for life, in all that you do
If you spend time and energy on the minor things
You'll not have room for that which happiness brings
The things that are important, which mean so much
Look after the golf balls first, keep in touch
Set priorities – remember the rest is just sand'
After this sound advice, one student raised his hand
'Sir,' he said, 'I noticed in all that you had to say
You didn't explain what part two beers play'
The professor smiled, 'however full your life is, my dears
You'll find there's always room for a couple of beers!'

JOURNEY INTO SPACE

Thorngumbald Young Farmers
On a journey into space
Encountered friendly aliens
And addressed them face-to-face.

'Greetings, we're from planet Earth
Young Farmers, here to visit you
We've swapped our tractors for a spaceship
Our members are the crew.'

'We've cast aside our overalls
Caps and wellies too
Left all our farms behind
To express our point of view.'

'We couldn't bring our stock with us
No cattle, sheep or pigs
We've left our crops all growing
And rented out our digs.'

'The pubs will all be empty
The dance floors deserted too
Charities, shows and competitions
Will be wondering what to do.'

'We all work hard, and play hard
Have fun in everything we do
So we've travelled on this spaceship
To share it all with you.'

An alien stepped forward
The leader, to be sure
He spoke in perfect dialect
Clear, concise and pure.

'Greetings, Thorngumbald Young Farmers
Your lives sound fun-packed, and full
But we think you must be spaced out
WHAT A LOAD OF BULL!'

In celebration of 50 Golden Years
Thorngumbald Young Farmers Club
1954 – 2004

WHAT'S PALE PINK?

I have a question
Do you know by chance?
What's pale pink
And hangs out Matthew's pants?
I don't mean to shock
Or render you quite dumb
But the answer is obvious
Of course it's me, his mum!

LITTLE BROTHER

Little brother, go away, I do not want to play
My friends don't want you either, so why not go away?
Just because I'm your big sister, and Mummy says I should
Doesn't mean I have to always be so good!

You're far too small to play with us; you just get in the way
You pester us and make a fuss, and shadow us all day
I wish that we could lose you, go away, I say
When you're a little bigger, then you can gladly stay.

Little brother, please don't cry, I know I was unkind
All right, you can play with us, my friends don't really mind
Close your eyes, count to ten, we'll play Hide and Seek
(Then, when your back is turned, away we'll quickly sneak!)

THE FARMER AND HIS HAYSTACK

The farmer, building a haystack, for his cattle's winter-feed
Decided, on the safe side, to stack more than he might need
He built it extra high, then summoned his youngest son
'Go to the Indian Reservation and see Chief Rising Sun
Ask him: What's in store for us? What winter will be like?
See if I should stack more hay,' he requested little Mike
Mike then left his father, heading for the Reservation
Chief Rising Sun greeted him, and gazed far in contemplation
'Bad winter,' he predicted, as he dolefully shook his head
Mike returned to break the news, from which his action led
To more layers on the haystack, ensuring cattle could be fed
But very soon, the farmer, still doubtful in his head
Despatched his son again, on an update he relied
Chief Rising Sun gazed afar, 'Bad, cold, snow,' he sighed
Which brought about more layers, the haystack rising high
Mike soon sought another forecast, with winter heading nigh
Chief Rising Sun gazed long, 'News not good,' he said
'Winter cold, snow, heap bad,' he solemnly shook his head
Mike stood in wonder, impressed and quite awestruck
'How can you predict such things, when far ahead you look?'
The Chief pointed out before him, the horizon they could see
'White man build big haystack, that's good enough for me!'

POLLY PUTS THE KETTLE ON

Polly puts the kettle on
To make a cup of tea
Sukie takes it off again
There's no electricity!

Polly sets the iron up
It'll only take an hour
Then Sukie reminds her
They haven't any power!

They think they'll watch TV
Until it is restored
But they keep forgetting
They have a lifeless cord!

Polly then suggests
They hoover up the floor
Put the washer on
And use the time in store.

But everything's impossible
With no power, you see
So they sit there doing nothing
Waiting for electricity!

THE WELSH SIGNPOST

LLANFAIRPWLLGWYNGYLLGOGERYCHWYRNDROB-WLLLLANTYSILIOGOGOGOCH

This signpost in Wales, the couple chanced to see
'Let's go there,' said Beth, to her husband, Lee
As he drove the car, the pronunciation, he tried
But she just laughed, as he got tongue-tied
A debate ensued, for neither could agree
Each with mind set on the way it should be
They stopped at a restaurant, in town, for dinner
The issue must be settled to establish a winner
Beth asked, 'Please pronounce just where we are
My husband and I are differing by far'
The cashier rolled her eyes, and slowly said
'Mac-don-alds,' incredulously shaking her head!

THE MOST BIBLES

'There was,' Jock told his mate
'A salesman, who stammered
Having sold the most bibles
His colleagues, he'd hammered
He won the sales prize
Defeating them all
By selling all his bibles
On door-to-door call'
'How can a man who stammers
So profusely bad
Manage to sell the most
And all the bibles he had?'
Jock's mate was confounded
'It doesn't make sense'
Jock said, 'It's no setback
He's far from dense
His sales pitch was slow
But persuasive too
Will you purchase a bible
Or shall I read it to you?'

THE GOLFER'S TEES

Jacko, the famous golfer
Well known was his name
Drove into a petrol station
Just prior to a game
He filled his Merc with fuel
But as he prepared to pay
He dropped two wooden tees
Which slowly rolled away
The attendant saw this happen
As he fulfilled his task
'What are they for, Jacko?'
He felt compelled to ask
'Putting my balls on while driving'
Said Jacko with a grin
'Wow,' said the attendant
'Don't Merc think of everythin'!'

SCOLDING CHIMP!

Two chimpanzees in a bath
'Ooh, ooh, ooh'
One was squealing loudly
As chimps are prone to do
The other scolded crossly
His patience nearly gone
'If your bum is scalding
Turn the cold tap on!'

WHAT A VIEW!

With our house on the market
It was likely we knew
When the doorbell rang
It would be someone to view
'Oh, no!' cried mum
'There's someone at the door
The house is a mess
Quickly drop to the floor!'
We followed her instruction
Five of us all
Each spread-eagled
Lying still in the hall
We quietly waited
For signs of retreat
But a key in the lock
Made our hearts beat
There we were discovered
Lying flat on the floor
As Estate Agent and client
Stared, each with dropped jaw!

THIS BRICK, THAT WATCH!

'You lad,' called the policeman
His delivery short and quick
'What are you doing
By this Jewellers with a brick?'
The lad knew he'd been caught
And begrudgingly replied
'I'm stealing that watch
When I've hurled this brick inside!'

The policeman grabbed the lad
Pushing him against the wall
The lad was shaking at his roughness
An action to appal
'Lad, you'll be in trouble,' said the cop
'If you don't do as I say
Hurl this brick, get *me* that watch
Then you can run away!'

THE DRUNKEN TOFF

The drunken toff
Hunting with his gun
Shot at a bird
On the run
With eyes unfocused
In his head
He managed to hit
A frog instead
Convinced he'd succeeded
The drink deceived
The lifeless frog
He then retrieved
'Amazing!'
Mused the drunken toff
'I've blasted
All its feathers off!'

BATTY!

Bruno and Boris were bats
Out hunting for a feast
Boris came back hungry
His futile search had ceased.

Bruno returned, licking his lips
Blood oozing from his fangs
'Where did you get it?' asked Boris
Suffering hunger pangs.

'Not even a mouse could I find
Come on, you have to show me'
They left the belfry together
And flew over dale and lea.

Soon Bruno slowed to a hover
And pointed to an enormous tree
'You see that, don't you, Boris?
'Well, I didn't!' he said mournfully.

THE CLOSEST SHAVE!

Freddie was in the barber's shop
Seeking a closer shave
'Better than I've ever had'
He requested Barber Dave
Dave had the perfect means
Two small wooden balls he placed
Between Freddie's cheeks and gums
The closest shave he faced
Indeed they were effective
Freddie was impressed
Then a question occurred
Which had to be addressed
'What if I swallow these balls?'
Dave thought, 'What a geek'
'Do,' he said, 'what everyone does
Bring them back next week!'

WIFE STRIFE!

James, a wealthy businessman
Rang home to his wife
But the maid responded
Which was to cause him strife
Tactlessly, she informed him
His wife couldn't take his call
She was entertaining her lover
A fact that did appal
James immediately ordered
The maid to take his gun
Pull the trigger on the pair
(That would spoil their fun!)
The maid left him on the line
He presently heard a shot
On her return, she confirmed
Her target had been got
One blast from James's gun
Had killed the pair quite dead
'Where shall I put them?
They can't stay in your bed!'
The maid asked for guidance
James then calmly said
'Dump them in the fishpond
To my piranhas, they'll be fed'
'But sir,' exclaimed the maid
'There are no piranhas here!'
'Oops! Wrong number,' said James
'I'm sorry I bothered you, dear!'

GET UP AND GO!

I'm lying in bed
Rubbing sleep from my eyes
I should get up and go
Greet the sunrise
But I'm not ready
To abandon my bed
With mundane chores
And tasks up ahead!

I'm still feeling tired
Is there a reason why
I can't linger a bit longer
And cosily lie?
Warm and snug
Idle and carefree
No reason at all
Except the duty in me!

With chores threatening
Like a big black cloud
This feeling of pressure
Should not be allowed
But of energy and strength
I am quite bereft
My get-up-and-go
Has got up and left!

THE ULTIMATE TEST

Three SAS recruits were taking the ultimate test
Knowing, on the outcome, their futures all would rest
Each were asked to prove his love for country, over wife
Take a gun and shoot her, the love of his life
The first two recruits reneged; they could not fulfil this deed
And withdrew from the test, knowing they'd failed to succeed
The third recruit took the gun and duly left the room
Shortly after, a shot was heard, all around felt gloom
Then came a smashing noise, and a woman's scream
Soon the recruit returned, quite breathless to extreme
He placed the gun on the table, with a big broad grin
The examining officer asked, 'What was all that din?'
The recruit, eyeing the gun, puffed, 'Only blanks in there
So, to death, I had to beat her, with a wooden chair!'

PICK SICK!

'Today Teddy is very angry'
Advised Looby Loo
'He's been working on a building site
A handy job to do
But someone stole his pick
Which rendered him annoyed
He could not do his job
Now he's unemployed'
'So sadly,' Looby Loo said
'He fair feels sick, and licked
Because today's the day
Teddy Bear had his pick nicked!'

CALLING THE DEAF!

After consulting his doctor
Lenny ventured to say
'I think my wife's going deaf'
The doctor was quick to convey
'Try testing her hearing
Then come back to report'
Lenny tried that evening
As he opened the port
'What's for tea?' he asked
As she stood at the sink
But she didn't respond
He poured out the drink
Then moved a little closer
Just behind her he stood
Repeating his question
But the response was not good
He moved forward again
Until right by her side
'What's for tea?' he called
Then she impatiently cried
'Lenny, what's wrong with you?
Don't you listen to me?
For the third and last time
It's chicken for tea!'

GOOD NEWS, AND BAD!

'I've got good news, and bad
I've been a naughty lad'
Said her husband, home early from work
'I've met someone new
So I'm ditching you'
He said with a cocky smirk!

'I'm packing my bags
I'll be leaving today'
He continued, as she threw him a smile
'That's good news'
She was quick to admit
'The best I've had for a while!'

'Now what's the bad news?
You better be quick
Hurry, say what you've come to say
I've a guy from the town
Who's coming right down
He's moving in later today!'

IN THE COFFIN WITH BERT!

Three grieving retired men
Bidding farewell to their friend
Stood beside his open coffin
Each there to the end
The first, a devout farmer
Believed it fitting and right
To leave money with Bert
For his final journey that night
He placed a twenty-pound note
In the coffin with Bert
The used car salesman agreed
And passed another note to insert
The estate agent paused briefly
Then thought, 'What the heck'
He exchanged the cash in Bert's coffin
For a sixty-pound cheque!

FAMILY PLANNING!

Discussing family planning
The newlywed gave her view
Three children, she would like
But her husband wanted two
'That would be plenty'
He said, 'quite enough'
A discussion ensued
The going got tough
'I'll have a vasectomy
After the second,' he said
His bride then implored
As she mulled in her head
Her new husband's wish
She could not condone
'Then *please* love the third child
As much as your own!'

TRAVELLING TROOP

Commando training was new to Private Lee
His superior advised, 'We'll travel by LPC
The next camp is twenty-five miles away
We'll start our journey at light of day.'

'What type of vehicle is an LPC?
It sounds impressive,' said Private Lee
His superior laughed, with shrieks and hoots
'Leather Personnel Carriers are walking boots!'

WEEPING WILLOW

When Willow weeps it's not hard to see
Why unhappy she might sometimes be
In summer when mighty temperatures soar
She's laden with leaves, too hot for sure
Then when winter brings the cold to bear
She's left quite naked standing there!

TEETH GRIEF!

'Go and clean your teeth, Kate,' said mum, with a smile
The four-year-old departed and was gone for quite a while
Presently, she returned with her puppy by her side
Her sparkling white teeth evident, as she opened wide
'Very good,' said mum, 'but the time you took was great'
'I cleaned puppy's teeth as well,' explained little Kate
Her shocked mum went shopping and brought a
  toothbrush back
A new one for Kate, and replaced it in the rack
She explained to her daughter, 'Use this one just for you
Not for cleaning puppy's teeth, it's not the thing to do'
Kate was emphatic, 'I didn't use my brush,' she said
'That would be disgusting, it was yours I used instead!'

A SWEET GESTURE

Tilly was most generous; rewarding those who came her way
The ones who showed her kindness, and helped her every day
She would carry sweets, to offer with grateful thanks
Showing her appreciation to the ever helpful ranks
Today was no exception, when shopping, Tilly stood
While the kind man on the checkout did everything he could
Of course she must reward him, a sweet ready in her hand
She slipped it across the counter, by the till to land
He politely refused, but she would not accept defeat
He finally gave in and consumed the offered sweet
Later, at home, while putting shopping in a drawer
She glimpsed her till receipt, then stared at it in awe
There, clearly registered, was the sweet she gave away
Three pence for confectionary from the 'pick & mix' display!

MY BEST POEM

It was my best poem
I thought it very good
The editor would accept it
I knew he really should
Print it in his magazine
Where all the world could see
That the greatest poet ever
I was destined to be!

Pompous and arrogant
I duly wrote to say
I'd other irons in the fire
So he should not delay
Received with the reject slip
His advice I thought a sin
'You should take the irons out
And throw the poem in!'

STUNNING GRACE

He met her at the seaside; it was a perfect day
As he dozed upon the jetty, she quietly swam his way
She splashed in the water, his attention she caught
A vision of beauty before him, the one he truly sought.

He fell in love at once with this girl, with tresses long
Golden curls cascading, his feelings were so strong
Her blue eyes met his; she was a wondrous sight
He had dreamed so often, this girl was truly right.

Her smile was so enchanting, though she never spoke a word
He beckoned her to join him, emotions all a-stirred
He leaned from the jetty, to gently take her hand
But she swiftly withdrew, preferring sea to land.

It was then he discovered this love could never be
A perfect alliance, deriving from the sea
For she was a mermaid; as she dived with stunning grace
He woke from his dream, when the water splashed his face!

THE SCHOOL INSPECTOR'S VISIT

The school inspector, in the classroom, addressed a little lad
'Who blew down the walls of Jericho?' was the question he had
'It wasn't me, I didn't do it,' the boy was quick to deny
The inspector was shocked and challenged the head nearby
'That young man is honest, I know it wasn't him'
The head defended the boy, the inspector looked quite grim
He then reported the issue to the education chief
Thinking this school would surely come to grief
But the chief's response made the inspector stare
'If they provide an estimate, I'll authorise repair!'

FED UP WITH THE MESS!

I'm fed up with the mess
It's a greeting I abhor
Newspapers scattered everywhere
Towels upon the floor
Dirty laundry cast about
Never in the bin
I can stand it no longer
This really is a sin!

I'm fed up with the mess
Sink full of dirty pots
On returning from work
Before my eyes, black spots
Tidy's not a word
That's recognised at all
This house is a sloppy sight
One that does appal!

I'm fed up with the mess
But I should not complain
The fact would be unaltered
With not a thing to gain
The mess, you see, is mine
And all mine alone
There's no one else to blame
I live here on my own!

FRUITY FRIENDS!

‘Sharing the same bed, my fruity friend
Has brought us both to this sticky end
Together, in sugar sweet sorrow, we cram
Preserved as a dollop of strawberry jam!’

FAR A-WEIGH!

One drunk asked another, in the pub, one day
'As a newborn baby, how heavy did you weigh?'
Tom garbled, 'I was only one and a half pound'
'Did you live?' asked Bob, slipping to the ground
'Did I live?' faltered Tom, as he mopped his brow
Proudly, he slurred, 'You should see me now!'

HEALTHY STUFF!

Mum was encouraging a healthy eating plan
On chips and fatty food, she had placed a ban
Cereals, fruit and vegetables, the option from now on
No white bread, just wholemeal; all other choice was gone
For her sons, this regime was proving very tough
They were objecting, and cutting up quite rough
As she stuffed a chicken, for much later in the day
The boys were brimming, with what they had to say
'We want sweets, and crisps, and biscuits,' they said to mum
'Not all this healthy stuff' - they were feeling glum
Mum then took two brown eggs, hoping to appease
'Come on, lads,' she said, 'these eggs will surely please
They're your very favourite.' But the boys had a different view
'If they're wholemeal eggs,' they said, 'you can stuff them too!'

THE SIGN ON THE DOOR

The vicar was pleased with the sign on the door
He aimed to attract people to church once more
It read, '*If you're tired of sin, please step this way*'
But he soon discovered, to his dismay
Someone had appended to the sign on the door
'*If not, ring Bess on six, two, double four!*'

HOLLY HOOT!

A small Christmas pud
With traditional sprig of holly
Was sent to friends in France
To make their season jolly
But their note of thanks
Had us laughing 'til we cried
'The lovely plant, though watered'
They said, 'had sadly died!'

TWO ESKIMOS

Two Eskimos in a kayak
As cold as could be
Desperate for warmth
Quite frozen at sea
One struck a match
And set fire to the craft
The kayak melted
With action so daft
There's a moral to this tale
As a lesson, you can't beat it
You definitely can't have
Your kayak and heat it!

NAME SHAME!

Two old gents were chatting, after dinner, one day
With their wives, in the kitchen, clearing dishes away
Len said, 'We ate at a fancy restaurant last night'
Dick asked its name, but Len was in plight
He couldn't remember, and frowned, as he thought
'What's the name of that flower, for love, that is bought?
You know, the one with thorns, that's prickly to pick?'
'It'll be a rose, you are meaning,' swiftly answered Dick
'That's it!' Len called loudly, so his wife could hear
'Rose, what's the name of that restaurant, dear?'

FOR HIS SWEETHEART

For his sweetheart's birthday, Ted wondered what to buy
Their relationship was new, and to please her he would try
He chose a pair of gloves, the finest in the store
He had them nicely gift-wrapped, which cost a little more.

Ted was not aware, but a mix-up then took place
A sexy pair of panties, in pretty pink, with lace
In error, he received, gift-wrapped and duly bought
Panties for his sweetheart, not the pair of gloves he thought!

His sweetheart, with the gift, received a note from Ted:

'Dear Sally, I chose these, just for you,' she read
'I notice you don't wear any, when I take you out
They're the shorter style, easier to remove, no doubt
The assistant advised, this shade herself would seek
She said they'd hardly soil if worn for many a week
She was so very kind; she tried yours on for me
You must show them off, wear them for all to see
I fear so many hands will touch them before I get a chance
Please wear them next Friday, when I take you to the dance
You must let me take them off, to kiss what lies within . . .'

Sally read no further, she threw the panties in the bin!

CAR-AZY!

Mark was stunned, his nostrils a-flare
As he stamped his foot on the floor
'How can my wife spot a blonde hair
But miss the garage door?'

FOREIGN EXCHANGE!

A foreigner changing yen for the pound
Was peeved at depreciation he found
Down a full ten pounds in a week
He queried the reason, in pique
'Fluctuations,' the teller told, true
He cursed, 'Fluk you Blittish too!'

THE CHAUFFEUR

Lord Hardy was interviewing
To recruit a new chauffeur
A replacement for Jeeves
Who was a bit of a loafer
'Come, take the Merc
Show me what you can do
Now tell me by what name
I should address you?'
The chauffeur hesitated
As they approached the car
'Call me James, sir,' he advised
'I would prefer it, by far'
Lord Hardy, ever mindful
Of standard etiquette with names
'I should call you by your surname'
He suggested to James
The chauffeur, on the issue
Quietly responded, in dread
'You can, if you insist, sir
But it's Darling,' he said!

A DAM SHAME!

Two fish out swimming, with no cares at all
Suddenly struck an almighty big wall
Both were stunned, and together screamed
'Dam!' they observed, and loudly blasphemed!

CHECKING OUT!

In the supermarket
Pam was checking where to pay
The *Express* lane no good
With trolley full today
The next was for *Disabled*
But she was fully fit
With no change, *Cash Only*
Would irk a little bit
Pam scanned the fourth lane
It surely must apply
Just then the assistant
Caught her roving eye
'You're nothing special, are you?'
Thoughtlessly, asked Pam
'Well,' replied the checkout girl
'My dad thinks I am!'

A PROMISE IS A PROMISE

Three pals, Tom, Harry and Dick
Set off for a walk, with a tasty picnic
After two hours, they arrived by a stream
In a field, among trees; very serene
Food and beer, they were quick to unpack
But something was missing; they were taken aback
No bottle opener; inadvertently left behind
Harry's pals pestered, if he'd be so kind
It would take four hours to return to base
A journey Harry was hesitant to face
Tom and Dick pledged faithfully they'd wait
Eat nothing until the return of their mate
Reluctantly, with solemn promises made
Harry agreed; he'd been finally swayed
Tom and Dick waited four hours, plus two
With no sign of Harry, and ravenous too
A promise was a promise, they both agreed
But their hunger was acute, in dire need
Under a tree, they prepared to cheat
Finally taking a sandwich to eat
Harry then dropped from the tree above
Scaring the pair, as he gave them a shove
'You broke your promise!' His anger was showing
'That does it,' he raged, 'I'm just not going!'

THE LAW OF DEDUCTION

'A most calculating figure was arrested today'
The policeman summed up, 'for his crime, he will pay
Caught with a ruler, setsquare and protractor
A slide rule and calculator, a damning factor
A public school teacher, he claims to be
But a member of the al-gebra movement is he
We're charging him, now we've made our deduction
For possessing weapons of maths instruction!'

ARMLESS DAN

'A pint of beer, please'
Requested armless Dan
Barman Pete obliged
He was a helpful man
'Now rummage my pockets
For money to pay'
Pete, Dan could see
Would have trouble that way
Dan then asked, if the beer
To his lips, he would pass
Again Pete obliged
Lifting up his glass
Dan sipped his beer
Then again had to ask
His white frothy lips
Prompting another task
'I've a tissue in my pocket
If you'd be so kind?'
'Of course,' said Pete
'I really don't mind
It must be difficult
Armless, as you are
To have to ask
For help in the bar'
'Yes,' said Dan
'It's embarrassing, you know
Now, where's the toilet?
I need to go'
Pete quickly pointed
'The closest, I fear
Is two streets away
We don't have one here!'

BUGGED!

James Bond was suspicious
Convinced without a doubt
His hotel room was bugged
They'd not catch him out
His enemies were many
And he knew the score
The element of danger
Was always at the fore.

As Bond had suspected
Beneath the bed he saw
An unusual device
Fastened to the floor
With specialist equipment
Taken from his case
He focussed his attention
To remove it from its base.

It took many minutes
Being firm and fast
But Bond's determination
Dislodged the thing at last
Within seconds he heard
A terrifying boom
As the crystal chandelier
Crashed in the dining room!

TOMMY, SHUT UP!

Auntie Freda waved goodbye to Heather and her boys
All three piled in the car, with their bags and toys
Heather drove away, with their voices ringing loud
'Mummy, mummy, mummy,' called her noisy crowd
'One at a time, please, in turn, you can have your say'
Tommy was most earnest, but he was waved away
'James can go first, then from you we'll learn
Tommy, please shut up, you must wait your turn'
Tommy was insistent, 'Mummy, let me speak'
'Not just yet,' she said – he was far from meek
James continued, as Tommy tried again
'Mummy,' he started, but it was all in vain
'Tommy, shut up, Paul now can have his say
For interrupting, your turn, I will delay'
Tommy fell silent, as Paul chattered on
Until, at last, after several miles gone
Tommy's turn arrived; he was free to speak
He'd tried to communicate; he was feeling weak
Taking a deep breath, he knew his words would scorch
'Mum, you've left your handbag in Auntie Freda's porch!'

COLD CREAM

Jenny's mum smoothed cold cream on her face, with care
As the little girl looked on, with eyes that turned to stare
'Mummy,' she asked, 'why put that stuff on your face?'
'To make myself beautiful,' said mum, 'it's a perfect base.'

Her mum then took a tissue and proceeded to dab
Wiping excess cream from her face, then came the stab
'What's the matter, Mum?' Jenny dared to ask
'Have you abandoned this truly hopeless task?'

ALL LIT UP!

Nighttime parachuting
Is a hazardous pursuit
So, many little lights
Are attached to every suit
Enabling team members
To pick each other out
A visual necessity
With darkness all about!

After one such exercise
The lost parachuting team
Knocked on a cottage door
The lady you might deem
On seeing her callers
Turned ashen in her fright
As she tried hard to focus
On this illuminated sight!

'Please tell us where we are'
The leading parachutist said
Her startled expression
Could easily be read
As they stood before her
All lit up in a clump
She bravely faced them
In her throat, a lump
Summoning extra courage
For all that she was worth
She trembled as she spoke
'You're on planet Earth!'

HERB PARDON

Herb in Bangkok
Was most apologetic
He'd not curry favour
Basil was apoplectic
'I've no thyme to cumin
I'll turmeric-shaw around
Go parsley and dale
Heading homeward bound
Rosemary will be waiting
With a tasty mint stew
Then I'll watch Coriander
Bit of Emmerdale too!'

FOR HER HUSBAND

'What's in your carrier bag?'
Enquired Jill, of Pru
'A bottle of fine red wine
I got for my husband, Stu'
Jill nodded in approval
Pru's choice wouldn't be a flop
'A bottle of wine for your husband
That's an excellent swap!'

SANTA'S GROTTY!

Santa's in his grotto
'Ho, ho, ho'
White beard flowing
Rosy cheeks aglow
'Hello, little girl'
He greets excited Jo
'Tell me your name'
But it's a major blow
Jo cries in disbelief
The magic ebbs away
'I told you when I saw you
In Durham yesterday!'

HIGH FLYER!

The sales rep was calling
On a farmer one day
Selling minerals for cows
As was his way
He was a high-flyer
The best in his trade
Confident, as ever
A sale could be made
The farmer was reluctant
But finally agreed
He'd see the sales rep
Though briefly indeed
'You've got five minutes'
Begrudgingly, he said
The sales rep was grateful
He nodded his head
Determined to cram
All he could in the time
He gave an excellent spiel
Clear and sublime
The farmer sat silent
As the rep had his say
Then looked at his clock
As the time ebbed away
'I like your approach'
Said the farmer, jaw set
'But your departure I'm sure
Will be better yet!'

THROBBING ROBIN!

Old Robin complained
To his doctor one day
'My right leg's throbbing
I'm in a bad way'
The doctor advised
'It's old age, I fear
There's nothing I can do
It's patently clear'
Old Robin retorted
As he limped out in a rage
'My left leg's all right
It's just the same age!'

IN A VACUUM!

In the science lesson
The teacher asked, 'Kim, dear
If you were in a vacuum
Do you think you'd hear
Noises from the outside
Penetrating in?
What would be your answer?
Would you hear a din?'
Kim, looking thoughtful
Gave a nervous cough
Then she asked her teacher
'Is it on or off?'

THE KIND CIVILIAN

Some soldiers, on exercise, were looking for a dummy
Someone to feign injury, and bandage like a Mummy
A kind civilian came forward, a healthy fit young man
As he lay down before them, the exercise began.

His head, they bandaged first, then his arms and legs
According to the proper First Aid rules and regs
Successfully accomplished, an ambulance stood by
Ready to transport this most obliging guy.

But one soldier was careless, as over him, he bent
His tin hat left his head and fell on the hapless gent
Whose skull was badly fractured, though they did not spot
the flaw
As they lifted him unconscious, and shoved him through
the door.

The ambulance drove off, at enormous speed, so fast
The kind civilian, inside, was tossed, and injuriously cast
The exercise, when completed, revealed conclusions to
astound
Under every single bandage, broken bones were found!

MANAGING ERNEST

'Why did you employ him?
It's a question I must ask
During our last meeting
I charged you with the task.

You must manage Ernest
Get him back on track
Or take drastic action
Give Ernest the sack!

Now you're telling me
His work is still the same
With no marked improvement
Like a duck that's lame!

He'll work if supervised
Or cornered like a rat
Otherwise he'll shun it
Like a lazy cat!

He's so disorganised
Constantly in a muddle
He'd be out of his depth
In a car park puddle!

When he opens his mouth
It's just to change his feet
He has no tact
And is seldom discreet!

Ernest comes in late
And leaves early every day
In between he'll sit and watch
The clock tick time away!

He sets low personal standards
Which he never achieves
He's no care for colleagues
Which generally peeves!

When others work with him
They are filled with gloom
He only brings them joy
When he leaves the room!

He's deprived a village
Of an idiot somewhere
He would argue with a signpost
He's such a useless spare!

He's a gross ignoramus
That's 144 times one
The wheel is still turning
But the hamster is gone!

Now our meeting's over
Your performance I decry
For not managing Ernest
I'm sacking *you* – goodbye!'

MY BUMP

I've a bump that's growing
Getting bigger every day
It can be quite tiresome
It's getting in the way
I have a hectic schedule
Now is not the time
I never wanted this
With dizzy heights to climb!

I'm not one for complaining
Far from it, in fact
But the issue is quite sensitive
And one requiring tact
I have told my partner
He doesn't seem to care
Anyway, we're breaking up
Love's no longer there!

I'm taking steps to purge it out
Get rid of it quite soon
I've a doctor's appointment
Tomorrow afternoon
I'm so very miserable
Now I need my mum
She's always there for sympathy
I've got a boil on my bum!

TODAY

Today is very special, my son has just left school
He's grown up tall and handsome, and is nobody's fool
His tie is all in shreds, his school shirt's quite a mess
His blazer's thin and worn, his trousers need a press!

His school bag's on the floor, with tattered books within
No more are they needed, destined for the bin
His coat and shoes cast off, lying all awry
With sports kit caked in mud, dripping wet nearby!

Through the years, these sights I've seen, many times before
Often aggravating, but today I'd wish for more
Tears I want to cry - he is my pride and joy
Today I've gained a grown-up son, but lost my little boy!

THE JOB APPLICATION FORM

My teenage son was completing an application form
He would not accept my help; I suppose it is the norm
Applying for a job, it was his first attempt
He'd do it all himself, he informed me with contempt!

When I saw what he'd written in the dotted space
In amusement, a smile crossed my maternal face
To tell him the true meaning, I wondered if I should
He'd answered: NEXT OF KIN: Mother
RELATIONSHIP: Very good!

THE UGLY DUCKLING

A young fledgling adopted by a family of ducks
Was cruelly teased for his ugly looks
How he differed, he didn't quite know
His heart was heavy, his ego low.

As time went on, the ducks still cast him out
He was sad and lonely, his sanity in doubt
He kept asking himself, should he run away?
If he wasn't like them, no more could he stay.

Approaching the lake, nervous and in fear
He looked into the water, his reflection was clear
But all thoughts of leaving were instantly gone
He *was* an ugly duckling, not a regal swan!

HER DIRTY SECRET

Ann called for her new boyfriend
The first time they'd been out
She was nervous, but excited
With butterflies about!
'John, it's lovely to see you
I'm glad you asked me out
But please may I use your loo
My tummy's giving clout!'
Ann was then embarrassed
She'd left an errant turd inside
She couldn't flush it out
No matter how she tried!
Then inspiration struck
She scooped it out in one
Wrapped it in a tissue
From the toilet, it was gone!
She stuffed it in her handbag
Calling out to John
'I won't be a minute
I'm putting make-up on!'
Together they went out
It was a lovely summer's day
Walking in the park
But crime then came their way
A man stole Ann's handbag
She was most distraught
As he ran off, by the lake
She hoped he'd not be caught!

But as luck would have it
John had trailed and found
Ann's handbag lying open
Abandoned on the ground
She was most distressed
Now her secret would be out
John would be disgusted
He'd ditch her, without doubt!
'Check the contents,' he advised
See if everything is there'
Ann looked inside her handbag
She hoped *it* wasn't there!
Her purse, with cash, was missing
But all else seemed intact
Except there was no sign of *it*
Such a pleasing fact!
With remaining contents gathered
Ann and John walked arm in arm
Through the park together
Ann felt relaxed and calm
But her discomfort wasn't over
On her left shoe, soft and dark
She trailed her dirty secret
Right across the park!

THE MAGICIAN AND THE YOKEL

Would you be surprised,' the magician mulled
If a rabbit from your pocket, I pulled?'
'I'd be amazed,' the yokel was quick to declare
'I happen to have a ferret in there!'

POOR BET

'I've had a really bad time,' said Bet to her friends
'I got Angina Pectoris, Psoriasis and Bends
Arteriosclerosis, Tonsillitis and Styes
Suffered Appendicitis, Diarrhoea and sore eyes
Hypodermics, they gave me; I nearly died!'
Bet's friends were sympathetic, shocked and wide-eyed
'However did you survive?' they asked poor Bet
'It was hard,' she said, 'the worst spelling test yet!'

DRIVING MOTHER

As a learner driver, taking my mother to church
Vast inexperience made the car wobble and lurch
The journey was long and uncomfortable, I admit
When we arrived at the church, she was ruffled a bit!

'Thank you,' she said, as she got out of the car
'My pleasure,' I responded, feeling better by far
But she slammed the door shut, with a succinct nod
'I wasn't speaking to you; I was talking to God!'

ALL BUSY!

On the emergency operator's line
There seemed to be nobody there
She redialled the number in haste
In case someone needed her care
A little boy whispered in answer
But denied he'd made the call
The operator asked, 'Where's mummy?
Can she speak at all?'
'No, she's busy,' he said
'She cannot come to the phone'
'Perhaps your daddy could come?'
She asked in a gentle tone
'No, he's busy as well'
Whispered the boy again
'What's your daddy doing?'
Her patience now on the wane
'Talking to the police,' he said
Timidly, she could tell
The operator was now aware
That all was far from well
'Please ask a policeman,' she urged
'To come and speak to me'
'Sorry,' said the little boy
'They're all far too busy you see
The firemen have just arrived
But they're all busy too'
The operator remained calm
Determined to see this through
'What is everyone doing,' she asked
'That so busy they be?'
The little boy whispered coyly
'They're all out looking for me!'

TOMORROW'S DINNER

Tomorrow's dinner in the oven, so organised, I thought
Chicken casserole, the dish, four fresh portions bought
To be cooked by 8.00 pm, before going for a swim
How could I forget? How could I be so dim?
At 9.00 pm, after many lengths were swum
I recalled the casserole, my body went quite numb
Spoiling in the oven, long past its cooking time
Tomorrow's dinner ruined, a culinary crime!
I sprinted from the pool, hot and in a sweat
Grabbed my mobile phone, from the locker, wet
Dialled the number home, my hubby to advise
He must take the chicken out, before its sad demise!
There was no response, so I called my son instead
He was in the pub, drunk out of his head
'Leave it to me, mum,' he drunkenly said
'I'll try to raise dad, or send big bruv instead!'
I returned to the pool to continue on my way
But visions of my casserole, all in disarray
Splattered round the kitchen, after exploding in the heat
Clouded concentration, my swim, I could not complete
I returned to my mobile, dripping and in distress
Praying tomorrow's dinner was saved from catastrophic mess
I rang home to my hubby, who answered this time round
He said, 'The phone's been busy, such a constant sound
Both sons were concerned that tomorrow's dinner's up in smoke
But you forgot to turn the oven on – is this a cooking joke!'

A GAPING HOLE

'I know we have a gaping hole
In our outside wall'
Said dad to little Charlie
'It's very clear to all
But as parents we're upset
For everywhere you roam
You're telling everyone
You're from a broken home!'

RICH BITCH

She'd become a woman of substance, with everything
A luxurious fur coat, a triple diamond ring
A plush Mercedes car, and yacht at sea
She was as rich, as rich, could be!

A home in the country and one abroad
Anything she wanted, she could now afford
But something she lacked, though was unaware
Her wealth was paramount, she did not care!

She had her health, and men falling at her feet
Lacking nothing, she thought, her life was complete
Her married lover, she'd extorted, a damning fact
The rich bitch was a blackmailer, scruples she lacked!

STANLEY'S CLONE

Stanley was a scientist, the creator of a clone
Another version of himself, exactly bone for bone
He took the clone to town, celebrating his success
But his action resulted in embarrassing distress.

Stanley's clone upset everyone they chanced to meet
He was rude and obnoxious; Stanley faced defeat
He tried to explain such behaviour was obscene
But the clone ignored him, his attitude was mean!

On the journey home, Stanley's mistake sunk in
He had to quickly rid himself of his invented twin
He pushed him off the cliff; of course, it was his right
Being his clone's creator, who could pick a fight?

But the police paid a visit; with knowledge of this fact
Stanley stood there wondering the reason for this act
'What's the charge?' he queried, when they came to call
'Sir, we're advised, you made an obscene clone fall!'

IN TROUBLE!

The aeroplane was in trouble
The pilot could see
His co-pilot was unmoved
Not worried was he
'My side engine's on fire!'
Cried the pilot, in fright
The co-pilot responded
'I'm lucky, sir, mine's all right!'

CROSS-EYED!

The man said to the vet
'My dog's cross-eyed'
The vet lifted the dog
No attention denied
After long examination
He turned the man's way
'I'll have to put him down
I'm sorry to say'
'That's a bit drastic
Don't you think?' asked the man
'He's only cross-eyed'
Now looking quite wan
'I have to,' said the vet
'You surely must see
He's such a big dog
So heavy is he!'

THAT SON OF MINE!

He's done it again
That son of mine
I'm in the bath
Just set to recline
But all is not right
On something I'm sitting
It's just not natural
And not very fitting!

Hard and spiky
Not inviting at all
That son of mine's
Enough to appal
I despair of the need
To tell him again
His habit is annoying
A definite pain!

Distasteful and offensive
Is this habit to me
That son of mine
I wish he would see
That he incurs my fury
In this aftermath
Of toe nail clippings
In the foot of the bath!

SPICED UP!

The man was unconscious
The prognosis looked bad
The doctor asked his mate
'What on earth has he had?
Was he smoking cannabis?
I need to be clear'
'Sort of,' said his mate
'But he used other gear
He ran short on stuff
And with tobacco too
He nipped into the kitchen
To add a spice or two
Turmeric and cumin
He rolled into a spliff
Will he be ok, doc?
He'll not be a stiff?'
The doctor sighed
'I think he'll live, for his sin
I'm fairly sure
It's a korma, he's in!'

PERCHED!

Tish and Tosh were parrots
Sitting on a perch
Tosh's eyes were active
Conducting thorough search
He was most agitated
Voicing his concern to Tish
'Is it my imagination
Or can you smell a fish?'

WHOSE PRETTY GIRL?

The little girl sat alone at the foot of the stairs
A house full of guests, the evening was theirs
A man entered the hall, and peered her way
Struck by her beauty, he had something to say.

'Whose pretty girl, are you, little girl?
With your lovely face, and hair all a-curl
The smile of an angel, eyes so blue
A picture of beauty - whose treasure are you?'

'Pretty girl, pretty girl, do tell me please
Whose little girl has looks like these?'
Tender love filled the face of the child
'Daddy, I'm yours!' the little girl smiled.

PASS THE PUD!

Jim's five-year-old daughter
Was helping serve the pud
She gave one to her father
It looked extremely good
Her dad politely passed it
To the lady on his right
Then she brought the next pud
And placed it in his sight
Again he passed it on
To another dinner guest
Returning with the third pud
She was not impressed
'You might as well keep this one'
She said with glaring eyes
'You'll not get a bigger slice
They're all of equal size!'

MY DADDY IS A MARTIAN!

My daddy is a Martian
Only you I'll tell
I'm the only one who knows
I've kept the secret well
Even mummy hasn't guessed
As I did long ago
Daddy's not aware
His secret I now know!

There are no outward signs
To show his Martian trace
No antennae visible
Pointed ears or orange face
He looks quite normal
No one would ever guess
That my daddy is a Martian
And really nothing less!

My daddy is a Martian
No one else has seen
It's my best-kept secret
The best there's ever been
Please don't tell a soul
I have to trust in you
Or everyone will know
That I'm a Martian too!

SEVEN YEARS BAD LUCK!

The mirror broke in pieces, shattered everywhere
He'd heard the consequences, enough to shake and scare
Seven years bad luck, he'd now have to endure
He'd heard this many times, he was alarmed for sure.

The first year he met a pretty girl and fell in love with her
The second year they got engaged; his emotions all a-stir
The third year he married her, in romantic style
Honeymooned abroad, cruised on down the Nile.

The fourth year he was promoted; his job was very good
Life for him was great, going as it should
The fifth year was special, his son was born you see
He could count his blessings, as they lived happily.

In the sixth year he won a fortune and wealthy became
Bought his own business and with it made his name
In the seventh year his daughter made his family complete
He knew he was a lucky man; he'd fallen on his feet!

He'd expected seven years bad luck, when the mirror broke
It was an old wives tale, which then had made him choke
But with seven perfect years, behind him and well gone
To ensure his luck continued, he broke another one!

WHAT BOTTLE!

I was next at the checkout, with a single bottle of gin
When an uncouth woman, with a full trolley, pushed in
She shrieked, 'I'm in a hurry,' as I stepped aside
My mouth agape, at the rudeness she'd applied
The assistant looked sympathetic, as she manned the till
She smiled at me, as the woman settled her bill
I put my bottle on the counter, but she winked and said
'It's taken care of, my dear, *she* paid instead!'

GOD IS WATCHING YOU!

The burglar froze in panic as he heard a voice
'God is watching you!' No time to rejoice
He dropped the TV in haste on his toe
Was his conscience calling? Should he quit and go?

As he turned to leave, from a corner in the room
He heard a parrot saying, 'Prepare to meet thy doom!'
'Oh, you're just a bird,' the burglar said relieved
Asking, 'What's your name?' as a sigh he heaved.

The bird instantly responded, 'I'm known as Carrot'
The burglar laughed, 'That's a daft name for a parrot
What idiot called you that?' he teased the bird with a prod
'The one,' said the parrot, 'who named the Rottweiler God!'

WHY WON'T HE COME SWIMMING?

Why won't he come swimming? It would help to get him fit
And serve to give him exercise, just a little bit
He admits it's what he needs, so why won't he come along?
He'd shed his excess body fat and make his muscles strong!

Why won't he come swimming? Does he think we would
    mock?
That the shape of his body would give us quite a shock?
Is he too shy and bashful, to join us in the pool?
Does he feel his swimwear makes him look a fool?

Why won't he come swimming? Would he feel undermined?
If he was a slower swimmer, afraid we'd be unkind?
Might we think it a weakness, if this was the case?
Would it dent his male ego to fall short on pace?

Why won't he come swimming? He has to admit
He would rather, fully clothed, at the poolside sit
He's not shy, or bashful, but it's really not for him
The reason, he says, is because he cannot swim!

AGE GAUGE

Chloe's great grandmother
Did not know her age
'Never mind,' said Chloe
'I know a way to gauge
Just look inside your knickers
That will tell you true
Mine say: *Age 10 years*
Yours will tell you too!'

A CLEVER PLAN

Nick and Mick, on a train, were impressed one day
To hear of a ticket scam, which ensured no need to pay
Two commuters boasted they travelled for the price of one
Hiding in the loo, then when summoned, staged a con
Just one ticket was submitted, which they slid beneath the
door
The inspector not suspecting they were out to break the law!

Nick and Mick planned next day to activate this scam
Destined to succeed, for it was a clever plan
On the train, they met just one man travelling that day
'There's only me,' he explained, 'my partner is away'
They divulged their intention, a single ticket bought
Confident the plan would work, no fear that they'd be caught!

'Today I have no ticket, but I've a clever plan'
The commuter explained - they marvelled at the man
As the inspector approached, Nick and Mick went to the loo
They hid behind the door, as they had planned to do
On hearing 'Ticket please,' they slid it underneath the door
Smugly, the commuter returned to his seat once more!

THE TEACHER'S CHALLENGE

'Now,' said the teacher, 'each Friday a question I'll define
He, who knows the answer, can take Monday to recline
What's the world's population?' she went on to ask
But no one knew the answer, impossible the task.

The following Friday, the teacher challenged her class again
'How many stars in the universe?' Of course, she asked in vain
Little Henry was tiring of such questions so unfair
He vowed to answer next week's, then on Monday not be there!

When Friday came at last, little Henry wriggled in his seat
Waiting for the teacher's challenge; this time it would be beat
As she was poised to ask her question, Henry was prepared
Releasing a frog from his pocket, as everybody stared!

It leapt towards the teacher; she expelled a sudden shout
'Whose frog is that?' she cried, nervous beyond doubt
Henry instantly responded, 'I've got the answer, miss - it's mine
I'll see you all next Tuesday - on Monday I'll recline!'

THEIR LOVE

Their love was so apparent everywhere they went
This union, they insisted, was truly heaven sent
Together, oblivious to everyone around
Safe in the knowledge their relationship was sound.

No one could come between them, their love was ever true
Still desperately intense, for it was all quite new
Some friends were in favour, other's not so sure
But romance was in the air, and nothing would it cure.

Their happiness together is so very hard to bear
My feelings once as theirs, when love was there to share
But my marriage now has faltered to a rueful end
For he is my husband and she's my former friend!

THE KING OF BERKS

On a train full of strangers, I observed a well-dressed gent
Obviously a businessman, whose action seemed quite bent
He was separating his newspaper, page by page
Crumpling each one carefully, it seemed to take an age
Then, in tight little balls, he threw them from the train
His activity made me curious; what could be his gain?
I approached him gingerly, 'Please may I ask
What you are doing? The reason for this task?'
He confidently replied, 'It keeps the wildebeest away'
'But there are no wildebeest here,' I felt obliged to say
Convinced this businessman must be the king of berks
Triumphantly, he responded, 'Which proves it really
works!'

DON'T THINK!

Don't think that I'm too good for you, don't turn from me away
Don't think that I've got talent, don't think that I will stray
Don't think my path in life will change, because I know it won't
Don't think I'll ever leave you, please don't ever, don't.

Don't think there'll be a limo to drive me to great fame
Don't think there'll be vast riches, lights around my name
Don't think I'll be a star, on radio, or TV
Don't think that's what's in store, for it will never be.

Don't think the media can tempt me, turn my head at all
Don't think, to the bright lights, they will loudly call
Don't think I'll resist temptation, I'll have to go and see
Don't think you can hold me back, you have to set me free.

Don't think you have influence, the bright lights beckon me
Don't think I'll stay at home, there's so much to do and see
Don't think it's just a dream, the glory and the fame
Don't think I won't enjoy it, I'm off to make my name.

Don't think you should blame me for adopting this view
Don't think it's fame and fortune that's driving me from you
Don't think my mind will change, ever firm it will stay
Don't think I won't return, I'll just try it for a day!

RON'S GOLF

Ron's golf was appalling, opinion he sought
His instructor advised how to develop his sport
'Ron, I strongly recommend you cut off a foot, or more
Shorten your golf clubs, you could do it with a saw'
'Will that improve my game?' asked Ron, desperate for a win
'No,' said his instructor, 'but they'd fit better in the bin!'

SITTING PRETTY

Sitting pretty in the meadow were Buttercup and Daisy
Gently swaying in the breeze, driving one another crazy
Daisy claimed she was the prettiest, with petals snowy white
She extolled her glowing features, so radiant and bright.

Buttercup, so vain, her golden petals shimmering in the sun
A picture of beauty, she thought she looked to everyone
She was the prettiest; she knew it was the case
Convinced her natural beauty outshone Daisy's pale face.

They sought an independent view, to settle the issue right away
They looked around the meadow for someone who would say
Who was the prettiest, the one who was most fair
Then a cow strolled up behind them and ate the pretty pair!

GOGGLED EYES!

I'd never have believed it, what a shock to my eyes
Wearing goggles for the first time, belief it defies
An eye-opener, a new dimension to swimming, I'd say
If I can't resolve this issue, I'll have to stay away!

The very thought of him, swimming close behind
His intrusive goggled eyes, I know I truly mind
What a sight he'll behold, beneath the waterline
I must avoid those prying eyes, or a new sport I'll define!

Now I've worked it out, if I zigzag across the pool
I'll avoid those goggled eyes, as a general rule
Though the lengths I swim may often clock a mile
I'll have doubled the distance, but truly cramped his style!

THE TRUCK DRIVER

The truck driver, on the motorway, could not believe his eyes
As he pulled up on the roadside, he gaped in sheer surprise
Strangely, a microwave looked dumped and all forlorn
He put it in the truck; his conscience was not torn
Several miles down the road, a police car called a halt
For his thieving action, he knew there was clearly fault
The PC asked the driver, who could not believe his luck
'Why is our speed-trap travelling in your truck?'

WATER!

Water in the reservoir
Water in the sea
Streams and rivers brimming
As full as can be
Water in the rainfall
Making puddles quite the norm
Ice, hale and snow
Into water will transform.

Water in the spring
Clean and fresh and cool
In the magic wishing well
And the swirling pool
Water, the life source
Of every living thing
There for us all to use
Comfort to bring.

Water, piped to our house
In a constant easy flow
Through taps, hot and cold
It's a blessing, we know
But with all this water in the world
Why is it regularly the case
That my young son never finds enough
To wash his hands and face?

MRS INDIA TYAS

Mrs India Tyas stepped on a drawing pin one day
For the remainder of the morning, there it was to stay
Securely lodged in her foot, a tight and cosy fit
She was unaware - it did not hurt a bit!

Her friend then spotted the drawing pin in her foot
She told her of its presence - she gave a little tut
Mrs Tyas pulled it out, the beginning of her doom
She instantly deflated, whizzing round the room!

HIS INTROVERTED BENT

Lonely and deprived
To the library Terry went
Seeking a book
To help his introverted bent
The perfect one he found
How to Hug its name
Borrowed from the library
Home with it he came.

But he was disappointed
When he looked inside
The contents were not
As the title had implied
Quite unexpected
With references so strange
It was Volume VI
In an encyclopaedic range!

LIKE MOTHER, LIKE DAUGHTER!

Jayne's parents were visiting their daughter one day
There, in the kitchen sink, a defrosting chicken lay
An upturned dish drainer was balanced on the bird
Dad looked at it curiously, his expression absurd
'What's that doing there?' He couldn't hazard a guess
How the dish drainer's presence would aid the process
Jayne looked to her mum, who was struck quite dumb
'That's the way *you* defrost chicken, isn't it, Mum?
I'm just following your example, what's wrong with that?'
Mum smiled blithely, 'But Jayne, *you* don't have a cat!'

MY VINTAGE WINE

'Taste my vintage wine, Dad,' I proudly invited
The results of which, I was highly delighted
An excellent sparkling homemade white
I thought I'd produced it precisely right
My dad raised his glass to me in salute
Surely its quality he would not refute
'Where's it come from?' he enquired of me
'The kitchen,' I responded, with infinite glee
His verdict shocked, as he shook his head
'Then it doesn't travel well,' he critically said!

THE SALESMAN

As the boy sat on the doorstep
A salesman called his way
'Is your mother in?' he asked
'I'd like to see her, if I may'
'Yes,' replied the boy
The salesman tapped the door
But nobody answered
The salesman spoke once more
'You said your mum was in'
The boy nodded to convey
'She is,' he reaffirmed
'But we live two doors away!'

THE RETIREMENT GIFT

The teacher was retiring
Leaving school that day
Her pupils were sorry
To see her go away
They brought her lovely gifts
To show how much they cared
They would really miss her
A sentiment she shared
First Tim gave his teacher
A gift wrapped in cellophane
His mother owned a flower shop
The contents were quite plain
Next Charlie presented
A pretty decorated box
His father owned a sweet shop
She unwrapped a box of chocs
Next came Joe, a strapping lad
Carrying for everyone to see
A large brown paper bag
The teacher looked in glee
Joe's father owned a public house
The best for miles around
His teacher anticipated
For whisky she was bound
He passed the package to her
His teacher thought it grand
But the contents were leaking
Dripping down her hand
She licked away the excess
As she released the tag
Then was disturbed to find
A puppy in the bag!

SHE'S JUST PERFECT!

She's practical and capable
Organised and warm
She'll keep her cool incessantly
And weather any storm
She's independent and ambitious
Creative with natural flair
Her knowledge and experience
With all she likes to share.

She's efficient and self-confident
As proficient as can be
Generous with her time
Popular and carefree
She's a charismatic person
With friendliness and charm
Always in a crisis
The one who's ever calm.

She's sensitive and versatile
Intuitive and true
Gentle, kind and honest
With the sweetest nature too
In fact, she's just perfect
There's no better one than she
I really can't dispute it
It's down on my CV!

THE FARMER'S PORCH

A tramp knocked on a wealthy farmer's door
'Please sir, I'm hungry,' he said, quite demure
I beg of you, give me something to eat'
The farmer was sympathetic, but not that sweet
'I never give anything for nothing,' he said
'I expect you to earn it, if you want to be fed
My porch needs painting, if you go round the back
Brush and paint, you will find, there is no lack
When you're done, a meal will be here for you'
The tramp was happy, this painting to do
An hour later, he was back at the farmer's door
'That was quick,' commented the farmer, 'for sure
Pull up a chair, you've earned something to eat'
The tramp was grateful and tucked into his meat
When fully nourished, his belly quite bloated
He raised a point on the porch job denoted
'By the way,' he advised, 'I should make you aware
I painted your Jag, because the Porsche wasn't there!'

DIY DAFT

Jack and Jill were do-it-yourselfers, ambitious and keen
Tending their new home, to decorate and clean
They painted and wallpapered, mopped and brushed
Scrubbed all the floorboards, until they were bushed
Falling into bed exhausted, after hard graft for days
In the darkness shone ghostly, silver light, rays
'Look, the moon's almost full,' Jill whispered to Jack
'I'll empty it tomorrow,' he groaned wearily back!

NEWS AFOOT!

The doctor, to his patient, came with news to relate
'I've bad and good tidings - I'm afraid, it can't wait
The bad news is, we've amputated the wrong foot
The other one, tomorrow, is due for the cut'
'So what's the good news, you wish to share?'
Enquires his poor patient, in utter despair
'The man in the next bed,' the doctor replies
'Wants to buy your slippers - he's just the right size!'

SNOW WHITE CONFUSED!

Snow White, with seven dwarfs
Was regularly confused
Their names she'd often muddle
Which rendered them amused
Many times each day
Their laughter could be heard
The dwarfs scoffing loudly
When mix-up occurred
One Sunday morning
After a heavy night before
When she and all dwarfs
Had been drinking until four
Breakfast was lunchtime
Only five dwarfs appeared
Snow White with a headache
For nonsense was not geared
She burst into the bedroom
To find the missing pair
Hiding under blankets
To confound her there
She cried, 'Please don't misbehave
When I'm feeling ropey
Dumpy, I'm appalled at you
For sleeping in with Gropey!'

A CLASSIC REVERSAL!

The graveyard, in Vienna, was peaceful and tranquil
Jeremy, passing through, then stood quite still
He could hear classical music, mysteriously played
Its origin he discovered, under a tree, in the shade
At the graveside of Ludwig van Beethoven, he stood
The Ninth Symphony, he heard, but not as he should
In reverse, it was playing, so puzzled was he
An explanation, he sought, what could it be?
Now, the Seventh Symphony, so clearly, he heard
Also playing backward, his emotions were stirred
Others then joined him; their curiosity grew
They'd heard the music, backward all through
Beethoven's Fifth Symphony began playing strong
More people were gathering, together in a throng
They stood at the graveside, as the Second Symphony relayed
Each perfect note, though always backward, was played
Beethoven's best works, in reverse order, composed
There had to be an explanation, they all supposed
Then the graveyard's caretaker appeared on the scene
Jeremy asked him, 'What does it all mean?'
The caretaker confirmed, he wasn't supposing
'There's no need to worry, he's just decomposing!'

PIZZA KING

Good King Wenceslas popped out
To the local diner
'Pepperoni Pizza please
Nothing could be finer'
The waiter approached his table
On this Feast of Stephen
'Your pizza, sire,' he said
'It's deep pan, crisp and even!'

WHAT A PICTURE!

Tom stood with his camera
On the beach by the sea
A lone man in his boat
Was bobbing carefree
A bather called, 'Wave!'
As Tom focused his shot
The man waved and smiled
Posing there on the spot
Quite blissfully unaware
A warning was defined
As the giant wave intensified
And engulfed him from behind!

PG'S TIP

PG was a taxi driver
To earn his crust each day
At the end of every journey
His passengers would pay
He was always obliging
For the tips he might secure
To encourage generosity
It worked he knew for sure
This night his fare embarked
After a very pleasant ride
'Have a drink on me,' he said
Slipping a tip inside
PG's top pocket bulged
It was extremely light
'Great,' he anticipated
'I've got a note tonight'
Peering into his pocket
He stared at it wide-eyed
In disbelief, there he found
A tea bag tucked inside!

PARACHUTE JUMP

It was Maxine's first jump; she was scared
Her instructor was confident she was prepared
'Remember all I've told you,' he reassured
'First, when you're ready, pull the big cord
If it doesn't work, the little cord's at hand
There'll be a red pick-up truck waiting when you land'
Maxine duly jumped and pulled the big cord
But nothing happened; it could not be ignored
She tugged at the little cord, but to no avail
'Just my luck,' she muttered, 'trust it to fail'
'I suppose,' she pondered, as rapidly she fell
'The red pick-up truck won't be there as well!'

HEART FELT!

The student nurse placed her stethoscope gently on the child
Deathly still, the little body, the nurse's pulse was wild
As parents looked on anxiously, she was torn apart
Not daring to admit, she couldn't hear her heart
Eyeing the child's face, she moved the stethoscope around
Praying her action would detect a beating sound
Then the child whispered, averting the student's fears
'Nurse, shouldn't you be wearing those things in your ears?'

MAD MARCH

On the first day of March
John rushed home from school
He was most upset
In floods of tears, a pool
'I worked really hard
I can't bear it,' wailed John
I've just learnt to spell *February*
Now it's passed and gone!'

MY CLEANER

My cleaner was quite elderly; she came most every day
To undertake the household chores, while I was away
Though sometimes she missed things, I put it down to age
She was quite forgetful; it was obvious to gauge.

I left her lists around the house of '*things to do today*'
To remind her of her duties, but it did not always pay
With tasks often left untouched and needing doing
The list grew ever longer and work just kept accruing.

Quite by chance, when I stayed at home one day
The window cleaner called; to him I had to say
On his last three visits, the master bedroom he had missed
Despite instruction to my cleaner to remind him on her list.

The window cleaner explained, embarrassed he had been
Up his ladder, with his bucket, the window set to clean
On his last three visits he felt it would have been a sin
To wake the lady on the bed, sleeping there within!

THE OPERATION

An operation needed, George was all prepared
He was feeling anxious, and really very scared
It was to change his life; of that there was no doubt
He was going into hospital, but soon he would come out.

No more playing rugby or drinking with his mates
Nor escorting pretty girls on romantic dates
He was leaving that behind from this very day
Well he understood it had to be this way.

The operation would render him more delicate than before
He had a positive outlook; he'd manage he felt sure
Aware life would be difficult, with changes to incur
New routines to follow, while causing quite a stir.

He'd have to change his job, but would take it in his stride
His disposition, he would no longer have to hide
Some friends would understand, others might be meaner
The operation was transforming George into Georgina!

STRAWBERRY DELIGHT!

Richard was delivering a load of manure
He queried with the gardener, 'What's it for?'
'To put on my strawberries,' the gardener explained
Richard looked surprised, his knowledge untrained
'At home we have strawberries quite supreme
But we don't put manure on, we use fresh cream!'

DRESSED TO KILL!

Jan's husband had been patient for an hour or more
As she tried on countless dresses in the fashion store
But he was tiring and wished she would decide
Which dress to purchase, with boredom hard to hide
When she next appeared, he looked at her in awe
'Yes, that's the one, this dress I do adore
You need look no further; it's a perfect fit
Stylish and elegant, sure to be a hit'
Horrified, and dressed to kill, Jan pushed him to the floor
'I was wearing *this* dress when we came into the store!'

THE FARMER'S WILL

The farmer had bequeathed his splendid flock of sheep
Seventeen fine animals, his three sons left to keep
Half his ewes to the eldest, one-third to the next
One-ninth to the youngest, which left his lawyer vexed
'How can this be done?' His clerk sensed his dismay
'It's just not possible to divide them in this way'
The clerk had the answer, 'I could bring my ewe
Then we'll have eighteen to give the sons their due
That's nine sheep for the eldest son, six for the next
Two for the youngest, according to the text
All seventeen sheep divided as the farmer did ordain
And I get to take my ewe back home again!'

TO GET TO HEAVEN

With Sunday school in progress
The vicar asked his crew
'If you want to get to Heaven
What do you have to do?'
Joseph put his hand up
'Pray a lot,' he said
'Be extra good, I think'
Suggested little Ned
Lucy said, 'Help others'
Nancy said, 'Don't lie'
Danny shrieked, 'You're all wrong
You surely have to die!'

THE ISLAND OF MY DREAMS

There's a special place, the island of my dreams
Where everything is perfect, with greenery and streams
Waterfalls and rainbows, sun and sea, and sand
Palm trees in abundance, a truly magic land.

I go to my island when I need to get away
When everything goes wrong, when I've had a trying day
Sometimes I go alone, to restore my peace of mind
Others, I crave company, and take it to unwind.

No one ever knows when and where I stray
My body may be with them, but my mind is far away
On the island of dreams, where I have supreme control
Living out my fantasies, achieving every goal.

It's the island of my dreams, the most perfect place
A haven for my fantasies, all sweetness and grace
But I'd never wish to make it real, that I truly know
As then, to live my fantasies, I'd have nowhere to go!

IN UNIFORM, GRAND

In uniform, grand, driving home from base
The pilot was left with a very red face
Out of fuel, he came to a halt
An oversight, it was his own fault
Leaving his car, he walked up the lane
Knocked at the first house, access to gain
'May I use your telephone?' he asked a young lad
'I'm right out of fuel, and late to my pad'
The lad stared at the pilot in uniform, grand
'Of course,' he said puzzled, 'but where did you land?'

PATIENT'S PATIENCE

I'm in the doctor's surgery waiting to be seen
My appointment time has long since come and been
I've listened to other patients' aches and pains and moans
And still the clock ticks on amid my disgruntled groans.

I've read all the magazines, impatiently tapped the floor
Stretched my legs several times, and paced the corridor
The clock's twice struck the hour; still I'm waiting here
The end of this patient's patience is drawing ever near.

People who came later have long since passed me by
Seen the doctor, got their pills, left in spirits high
Why am I forsaken? Is there something wrong with me?
Actually no longer, for time has healed me!

THE AMBASSADOR'S GIFT

'What would you like this Christmas?' asked the TV station
Addressing a high profile ambassador of this nation
'Truly nothing, I would like, for I could not accept'
He explained that a gift was unnecessary and inept
The TV station insisted his preference he should share
So reluctantly he suggested a gift he thought was fair
On Christmas Eve, days later, he switched on his TV set
Noting the results of the survey, he would soon regret
Unbeknown to him, his suggestion had been included
The TV station was responsible, the ambassador deluded
'The French ambassador has asked for peace on earth today
An end to war and suffering,' he heard the announcer say
'The German ambassador wants an upsurge in business trend
Growth and prosperity, which he hopes will never end
Finally, the British ambassador,' the TV announcer said
'Would really like, this Christmas, a pair of socks for bed!'

FROZEN TURKEYS

The supermarket was stocked
With frozen turkeys galore
The shopper examined
Every freezer for more
'Do they get any bigger?'
To the assistant, she said
'No, madam,' he replied
'Because they are all dead!'

THIRTY MEN, OR MORE!

At first, looking skyward, he stood there on his own
A young man came and joined him; he was no more alone
Without a word, he too looked up; collectively they peered
Another man approached, and looked up as he neared.

All three men now gazed up into the sky of blue
Then a fourth appeared and joined the vigilant crew
Number five, and six came forth, looking up as well
Others joined the little group, which made the numbers swell.

As time went by, there came, to stand, thirty men or more
Looking high above them, though no one knew what for
Then someone asked the first man, why they looked into the sky?
'I can't speak for them,' he said, 'but a stiff neck's my reason why!'

LIGHT WEIGHT!

The fat heavy man stood on the public scales
As the pointer went round, he expelled loud wails
It finally stopped at two and a half stones
He stood quite still, emanating groans
A passer-by stared intently with dropped jaw
'You must be hollow,' he exclaimed in awe!

GOT IT!

With wife in the kitchen preparing his tea
A hunger so dire was ravaging Lee
The TV was on; he sat comfy in chair
As the Lottery results unfolded there
'Got it,' he called, as the first number appeared
'That too,' he observed, as the second one cleared
The third number rolled out, then the next
He sat bolt upright, his fingers he flexed
He whooped as the fifth number was revealed
She, sensing his tension, from the kitchen reeled
Swiftly approached him, placed his meal by his side
Overwhelming excitement could not be denied
'Have we won?' she chirped as the last number was cast
'Course not,' Lee chuckled, 'I just wanted tea fast!'

A PARENT'S LETTER

Dear Scout Master
        I'm writing just to say
How much my son enjoyed his camp away
An activity weekend, packed with things to do
Hiking, abseiling, canoeing, just to name a few
What a wise suggestion, a plastic bag to pack
With the weather as it was, of rain there was no lack
Every bit of kit came home wringing wet
Except his neatly folded face flannel!
        Yours sincerely
        Mrs Lett

SLOW PROGRESS

He was late for the ferry
Just his luck
It was on the move
He was an agile buck
It was making slow progress
If he was quick
He knew a run and a jump
Would do the trick
So he took a short run
And a mighty leap
Landing on the deck
In a crumpled heap
Then he tripped as he rose
And the captain said with a grin
'We could have saved you that trip
We're coming in!'

GRANDAD'S SPECS

Grandad's lost his specs again
He searches high and low in vain
On the bookcase
Beneath the chair
On the table
But they're not there!
In the cupboard
On the shelf
Grandad chides his careless self
He looks in drawers
But to no avail
He needs his specs
To read the mail!

When he's looked everywhere
And all around
With still no specs
To be found
He's had his break
Had lunch and tea
Given up
For he can't see
Guess what! - Granny comes home
She finds them straight away
Perched high on his head
They've been there all day!

THE WAITER ASKED!

'Sir,' the waiter asked
'How did you find your steak?'
It was generally his custom
This enquiry to make
The diner responded
Through tight and gritted teeth
'I just rolled a pea over
And found it underneath!'

THE CHALLENGE

Strongman Jim could not believe the challenge put to him
He was sure the skinny stranger must be very dim
'A wheelbarrow, with something in, I'll push along the street
But you'll never push it back again, I'll bet you face defeat!'

Strongman Jim accepted the bet, for fifty pounds
Convinced the skinny stranger had stepped beyond his
bounds
With a wheelbarrow ready, and the challenge set to begin
The skinny stranger instructed, 'Now, strongman, please get
in!'

THANK YOU, MY FRIEND

Master of my mind, I'm glad our friendship has sustained
Throughout my third book, with me, you have remained
Penetrating my thoughts, committing words to rhyme
I'd be truly lost, if you could not spare the time.

I'd have no rhyme or reason to continue with my quest
If your inspiration was lacking, I could not do my best
I could no longer write, without my faithful friend
You're the master of my mind, stay until the end.

One more verse to write, then my book is done
The culmination of many hours of fun
Thank you, my friend, for your inspiration, true
Master of my mind, you know that I love you!

Printed in the United Kingdom
by Lightning Source UK Ltd.
101992UKS00001B/1-75

9 781843 751168